BAPTISMAL REGENERATION

𝔐etropolitan 𝔗abernacle 𝔓ulpit.

BAPTISMAL
REGENERATION

Delivered on Sunday Morning, June 5ᵀᴴ, 1864, by

Charles H. Spurgeon

at the Metropolitan Tabernacle, Newington.

Updated to modern language by Charles J. Doe

Minneapolis

Published by Curiosmith.
Minneapolis, Minnesota.
Internet: curiosmith.com.

Previously published by PASSMORE & ALABASTER in 1864.

The text of this edition is from sermon number 573, Volume 10 of *The Metropolitan Tabernacle Pulpit*, 1864.

The text was updated to modern equivalents of Elizabethan and Victorian words and phrases. Occasional occurrences of lengthy sentences and close punctuation were left unchanged.

Definitions are from *Webster's Revised Unabridged Dictionary,* 1828 and 1913.

The "Guide to the Contents" was added to this edition by the publisher.

ISBN 9781941281093

GUIDE TO THE CONTENTS

———◦◦⦂◉⦂◦◦———

BAPTISMAL REGENERATION

A SERMON BY

CHARLES H. SPURGEON

He said to them, "Go into all the world and preach the good news to all creation. Whoever believes and is baptized will be saved, but whoever does not believe will be condemned.—MARK 16:15–16 (NIV).

In the preceding verse our Lord Jesus Christ gives us some little insight into the natural character of the apostles whom he selected to be the first ministers of the Word. They were evidently men of like passions with us, and needed to be rebuked even as we do. On the occasion when our Lord sent forth the eleven to preach the gospel to every creature, he "appeared to the Eleven as they were eating; he rebuked them for their lack of faith and their stubborn refusal to believe those who had seen him after he had risen";[1] from which we may surely gather that to preach the Word, the Lord was

1 Mark 16:14 (NIV).

pleased to choose imperfect men; men, too, who of themselves were very weak in the grace of faith in which it was most important that they should excel. Faith is the conquering grace, and is of all things the main requisite in the preacher of the Word. Yet the honored men who were chosen to be the leaders of the divine crusade needed a rebuke concerning their unbelief. Why was this? Why, my brothers and sisters, because the Lord has ordained that we should always have this treasure in *jars of clay*, that the excellency of the power may be of God and not of us. If you should find a perfect minister, then might the praise and honor of his usefulness accrue to man; but God is frequently pleased to select for eminent usefulness men evidently honest and sincere, but who have some manifest infirmity by which all the glory is cast off from them and laid on himself, and on himself alone. Let it never be supposed that we who are God's ministers either excuse our faults or claim perfection. We labor to walk in holiness, but we cannot claim to be all that we wish to be. We do not base the claims of God's truth on the spotlessness of our characters, but on the fact that it comes from him. You have believed in spite of our infirmities, and not because of our virtues. If indeed, you had believed our word because of our supposed perfection, your faith would stand in the excellency of man and not in the power of God. We come to you often with much trembling, sorrowing over our follies and weaknesses, but we deliver to you God's Word as God's Word, and we ask you to receive it not as coming from us poor, sinful mortals, but as proceeding from the Eternal and Thrice Holy God. If you so receive it, and by its own vital force are moved and stirred up towards God and his ways, then it is the indisputable work of the Word, which it could not and would not be if it rested in any way on man.

Therefore our Lord has given us an insight into the character of the persons whom he has chosen to proclaim his truth, then goes on to deliver to the chosen champions, their commission for the Holy War. I ask you to note the words with solemn care. He sums up in a few words the entirety of their work, and at the same time foretells the result of it, telling them that some would doubtless believe and so be saved, and some on the other hand would not believe and would most certainly, therefore, be condemned, that is, condemned forever to the penalties of God's wrath. The lines containing the commission of our ascended Lord are certainly of great importance, and demand devout attention and implicit obedience, not only from all who aspire to the work of the ministry, but also from all who hear the message of mercy. A clear understanding of these words is absolutely necessary to our success in our Master's work, for if we do not understand the commission it is not at all likely that we shall discharge it correctly. To alter these words would be more than impertinence, it would involve the crime of treason against the authority of Christ and the best interests of the souls of men and women. May I have grace to be very vigilant here.

Wherever the apostles went they met with obstacles to the preaching of the gospel, and the more open and effectual was the door of utterance the more numerous were the adversaries. These brave men who wielded the sword of the Spirit put to flight all their foes. They didn't do this by skilled deception and deceit, but by making a direct cut at the error which impeded them. Never did they dream for a moment of adapting the gospel to the unholy tastes or prejudices of the people, but at once directly and boldly they brought down with both their hands the mighty sword of the Spirit upon the crown of the opposing error. This morning, in the name of the Lord of Hosts, my Helper and Defense, I shall attempt to do the same, and if I should provoke some hostility—if I should through speaking what I believe to be the truth lose the friendship of some and stir up the enmity of more, I cannot help it. The burden of the Lord is on me, and I must liberate my soul. I have been reluctant enough to undertake the work, but I am forced to it by a reverent and overwhelming sense of solemn duty. As I am soon to appear before my Master's bar, I will this day, if ever in my life, bear my testimony for truth, and run all risks. I am content to be cast out as evil if it must be so, but I cannot, I dare not, hold my peace. The Lord knows I have nothing in my heart but the purest love to the souls of those whom I feel imperatively called to rebuke sternly in the Lord's name. Among my hearers and readers, a considerable number will censure if not condemn me, but I cannot help it. If I forfeit your love for truth's sake I am grieved for you, but I cannot, I dare not, do otherwise. It is as much as my soul is worth to hold my peace any longer, and whether you approve or not I must speak out. Did I ever court your approbation? It is sweet to everyone to be applauded; but if for the sake of the comforts of respectability and the smiles of others, any Christian minister shall keep back a part of his testimony, his Master at the last shall require it at his hands. This day, standing in the immediate presence of God, I shall speak honestly what I feel, as the Holy Spirit shall enable me. I shall leave the matter with you to judge concerning it, as you will answer for that judgment at the last great day.

I find that the great error which we have to contend with throughout England (and it is growing more and more), is one in direct opposition to my text, well known to you as the doctrine of baptismal regeneration. We will confront this dogma with the assertion, that BAPTISM WITHOUT FAITH SAVES NO ONE. The text says, "Whoever *believes* and is baptized will be saved," but whether a person is baptized or not, it asserts that *"whoever does not believe* shall be condemned," so that baptism does not save the unbeliever, no, it does not in any degree exempt them from the common doom of all the ungodly. They may have baptism, or they may not have baptism, but if they do not believe, they shall be in any case most surely condemned. Let them be baptized by immersion or sprinkling, in their infancy, or in their adult age, if they are not led to put their trust in Jesus Christ—if they remain an unbeliever, then this terrible doom is pronounced upon them—"Whoever does not believe will be condemned." I am not aware that any Protestant Church in England teaches the doctrine of baptismal regeneration except one, and that happens to be the corporation which with none too much humility calls itself *the* Church of England. This very powerful sect does not teach this doctrine merely through a section of its ministers, who might charitably be considered as evil branches of the vine, but it openly, boldly, and plainly declares this doctrine in her own appointed standard, the Book of Common Prayer, and that in words so plain and clear, that while language is the channel of conveying intelligible sense, no process short of violent wresting[1] from their plain meaning can ever make them say anything else.

1 Wresting—pulling with a twist; distorting; perverting.

Here are the words—we quote them from the Catechism which is intended for the instruction of youth, and is naturally very plain and simple, since it would be foolish to trouble the young with metaphysical refinements. The child is asked its name, and then questioned, "Who gave you this name?" "My godfathers and godmothers in my baptism; in which I was made a member of Christ, the child of God, and an inheritor of the kingdom of heaven." Isn't this definite and plain enough? I prize the words for their candor; they could not speak more plainly. Three times over the thing is put, for fear that there should be any doubt in it. The word regeneration may, by some sort of juggling, be made to mean something else, but here there can be no misunderstanding. The child is not only made "a member of Christ"—union to Jesus is no mean spiritual gift—but they are made in baptism "the child of God" also. Since the rule is, "if children then heirs," they are also made "an inheritor of the kingdom of heaven." Nothing can be more plain. I venture to say that while honesty remains on earth the meaning of these words will not be disputed. It is clear as noon day that, as the Rubric[1] has it, "Fathers, mothers, masters, and dames, are to cause their children, servants, and apprentices," no matter how idle, giddy, or wicked they may be, to learn the Catechism, and to say that in baptism they

1 Rubric—directions printed in prayer books.

were made members of Christ and children of God. The form for the administration of this baptism is hardly less plain and outspoken, seeing that thanks are expressly returned to the Almighty God, because the person baptized is regenerate. "Then shall the priest say, 'Seeing now, dearly beloved brethren, that this child is regenerate and grafted into the body of Christ's Church, let us give thanks to Almighty God for these benefits, and with one accord make our prayers to him, that this child may lead the rest of his life according to this beginning.'" Nor is this all, for to leave no mistake, we have the words of the thanksgiving prescribed, "Then shall the priest say, 'We yield you hearty thanks, most merciful Father, that it has pleased you to regenerate this infant with your Holy Spirit, to receive him for your own child by adoption, and to incorporate him into your holy Church.'"

This, then, is the clear and unmistakable teaching of a Church calling itself Protestant. I am not now dealing at all with the question of infant baptism—I have nothing to do with that this morning. I am now considering the question of baptismal regeneration, whether in adults or infants, or ascribed to sprinkling, pouring, or immersion. Here is a Church which teaches every Lord's Day in the Sunday-school, and should, according to the Rubric, teach openly in the Church, all children were made members of Christ, children of God, and inheritors of the kingdom of heaven when they were baptized! Here is a professedly Protestant Church, which, every time its minister goes to the font, declares that every person there receiving baptism is there and then "regenerated and grafted into the body of Christ's Church."

"But," I hear many good people exclaim, "there are many good clergymen in the Church who do not believe in baptismal regeneration." To this my answer is prompt. Why then do they belong to a Church which teaches that doctrine in the plainest terms? I am told that many in the Church of England preach against her own teaching. I know they do, and in this I rejoice in their enlightenment, but I question, gravely question their morality. To take oath that I sincerely assent and consent to a doctrine which I do not believe, would to my conscience appear a little short of perjury, if not absolute downright perjury, but those who do so must be judged by their own Lord. For me to take money for defending what I do not believe—for me to take the money of a Church, and then to preach against what are most evidently its doctrines—I say for me to do this (I judge others as I would that they should judge me) for me, or for any other simple, honest man to do so, were an atrocity so great, that if I had perpetrated the deed, I should consider myself out of the pale of truthfulness, honesty, and common morality. Fellow members, when I accepted the office of minister of this congregation, I looked to see what were your articles of faith. If I had not believed them I should not have accepted your call, and when I change my opinions, rest assured that as an honest man I shall resign the office, for how could I profess one thing in your declaration of faith, and quite another thing in my own preaching? Would I accept your pay, and then stand up every Sabbath day and talk against the doctrines of your standards? For clergymen to swear or say that they give their solemn assent and consent to what they do not believe is one of the grossest pieces of immorality perpetrated in England. It is most pestilential in its influence, since it directly teaches men to lie whenever it seems necessary to do so in order to get a living or increase their supposed usefulness. It is in fact an open testimony from priestly lips that at least in ecclesiastical matters falsehood may express truth, and truth itself is a mere unimportant nonentity. I know of nothing more calculated to debauch the public mind than a want of straightforwardness in ministers. When worldly people hear ministers denouncing the very things which their own Prayer Book teaches, they imagine that words have no meaning among ecclesiastics, and that vital differences in religion are merely a matter of tweedle-dee and tweedle-dum,[1]

---

1 Tweedle-dee and Tweedle-dum—a reference to characters made popular in *Through the Looking-Glass* by Lewis Carroll, characterized by having few differences.

and that it does not matter much what a person does believe so long as they are charitable towards other people. If baptism does regenerate people, let the fact be preached with a trumpet tongue, and let no person be ashamed of their belief in it. If this is really their creed, by all means let them have full liberty for its propagation. My brothers and sisters, those are honest Churchmen who, in this matter, subscribing to the Prayer Book, believe in baptismal regeneration, and preach it plainly. God forbid that we should censure those who believe that baptism saves the soul, because they adhere to a Church which teaches the same doctrine. So far they are honest men, and in England, where else, let them never lack a full toleration. Let us oppose their teaching by all Scriptural and intelligent means, but let us respect their courage in plainly giving us their views. I hate their doctrine, but I love their honesty, and as they speak what they believe to be true, let them speak it out, and the more clearly the better. Speak it out, gentlemen, be what it may, but do let us know what you mean. For my part, I love to stand foot to foot with an honest foeman.[1] To open warfare, bold and true hearts raise no objection, but the ground of quarrel is covert enmity, which we have most cause to fear and best reason to detest. That crafty kindness which inveigles me to sacrifice principle is the serpent in the grass—deadly to

1 Foeman—an enemy in war.

the incautious wayfarer. Where union and friendship are not cemented by truth, they are an unholy
confederacy. It is time that there should be an end
put to the flirtations of honest men with those who
believe one way and swear another. If men believe
baptism works regeneration, let them say so, but
if they do not believe it so in their hearts, and yet
give their consent, and yet more, get their livings
by consenting to words asserting it, let them find
congenial associates among men who can equivo-
cate and shuffle, for honest men will neither ask
nor accept their friendship.

We ourselves are not dubious on this point, we
protest that persons are not saved by being baptized.
In such an audience as this, I am almost ashamed
to go into the matter, because you surely know better than to be misled. Nevertheless, for the good of
others we will drive at it. We hold that persons are
not saved by baptism, for we think, first of all that
*it seems out of character with the spiritual religion
which Christ came to teach*, that he should make
salvation depend on mere ceremony. Judaism might
possibly absorb the ceremony by way of type into
her ordinances essential to eternal life, for it was
religion of types and shadows. The false religions of
the heathen might inculcate salvation by a physical
process, but Jesus Christ claims for his faith that it
is purely spiritual, and how could he connect regeneration with a peculiar application of aqueous fluid?

I cannot see how it would be a spiritual gospel, but I can see how it would be mechanical, if I were sent forth to teach that the mere dropping of so many drops upon the brow, or even the plunging a person in water could save the soul. This seems to me to be the most mechanical religion now existing, and to be on a par with the praying windmills of Tibet,[1] or the climbing up and down of Pilate's Staircase[2] to which Luther subjected himself in the days of his darkness. The operation of water-baptism does not appear even to my faith to touch the point involved in the regeneration of the soul. What is the necessary connection between water and the overcoming of sin? I cannot see any connection which can exist between sprinkling, or immersion, and regeneration, so that the one shall necessarily be tied to the other in the absence of faith. Used by faith, had God commanded it, miracles might be performed, but without faith or even consciousness, as in the case of babes, how can spiritual benefits be connected necessarily with the sprinkling of water? If this be your teaching, that regeneration goes with baptism, I say it looks like the teaching of a spurious

---

1 Praying windmills of Tibet—A wind-driven prayer wheel that, according to tradition, would automatically pray for a person as it turns.

2 Pilate's staircase (Scala Sancta)—claimed to be Pontius Pilate's stairs that Christ traversed. A pope granted an indulgence to reduce time in Purgatory, if climbed on the knees.

Church, which has craftily invented a mechanical salvation to deceive ignorant, sensual, and grovelling minds, rather than the teaching of the most profoundly spiritual of all teachers, who rebuked Scribes and Pharisees for regarding outward rites as more important than inward grace.

But it strikes me that a more forcible argument is that *the dogma is not supported by facts*. Are all persons who are baptized children of God? Well, let us look at the divine family. Let us notice their resemblance to their glorious Parent! Am I untruthful if I say that thousands of those who were baptized in their infancy are now in our jails? You can ascertain the fact if you please, by application to prison authorities. Do you believe that these people, many of whom have been living by plunder, felony, burglary, or forgery, are regenerate? If so, the Lord deliver us from such regeneration. Are these villains members of Christ? If so, Christ has sadly altered since the day when he was holy, harmless, undefiled, separate from sinners. Has he really taken baptized drunkards and harlots to be members of his body? Do you not revolt at the supposition? It is a well-known fact that baptized people have been hanged. Surely it can hardly be right to hang the inheritors of the kingdom of heaven! Our sheriffs have much to answer for when they officiate at the execution of the children of God, and suspend the members of Christ on the gallows! What a detestable farce is that which is transacted at the open grave, when "a dear brother" who has died drunk is buried in a "sure and certain hope of the resurrection of eternal life," and the prayer that "when we shall depart this life we may rest in Christ, as our hope is that this our brother does."[1] Here is a regenerate brother, who having defiled the village by constant foulness and vile drunkenness, died without a sign of repentance, and yet the professed minister of God solemnly accords him funeral rites which are denied to unbaptized innocents, and puts the reprobate into the earth in "sure and certain hope of the resurrection to eternal life." If old Rome in her worst days ever perpetrated a grosser piece of imposture than this, I do not read things rightly. If it does not require a Luther to cry down this hypocrisy as much as Popery[2] ever did, then I do not even know that twice two make four. Do we find—we who baptize on profession of faith, and baptize by immersion in a way which is confessed to be correct, though not allowed by some to be absolutely necessary to its validity—do we who baptize in the name of the sacred Trinity as others do, do we find that baptism regenerates? *We do not.* Neither in the righteous nor the wicked do we find regeneration brought about by baptism. We have never met with one

---

1 A quote from *Anglican Book of Common Prayer*.
2 Popery—the religion of the Roman Catholic Church, comprehending doctrines and practice.

believer, however instructed in divine things, who could trace his regeneration to his baptism, and on the other hand, we confess it with sorrow, but still with no surprise, that we have seen those whom we have ourselves baptized, according to apostolic precedent, go back into the world and wander into the foulest sin, and their baptism has hardly been so much as a restraint to them, because they have not believed in the Lord Jesus Christ. Facts all show that whatever good there may be in baptism, it certainly does not make a person "a member of Christ, the child of God, and an inheritor of the kingdom of heaven," or else many thieves, prostitutes, drunkards, fornicators, and murderers, are members of Christ, the children of God, and inheritors of the kingdom of heaven. Facts, brothers and sisters, are against this Popish doctrine, and facts are stubborn things.

Yet further, I am persuaded *that the performance styled baptism by the Prayer Book is not at all likely to regenerate and save.* How is the thing done? One is very curious to know when one hears of an operation which makes people members of Christ, children of God, and inheritors of the kingdom of heaven, how the thing is done. It must in itself be a holy thing truthful in all its details, and edifying in every portion. Now, we will suppose we have a group of people gathered around the water, be it more or less, and the process of regeneration is about to be performed. We will suppose them all to be godly people. The clergyman officiating is a profound believer in the Lord Jesus, and the father and mother are exemplary Christians, and the godfathers and godmothers are all gracious people. We will suppose this—it is a charitable supposition, but it may be correct. What are these godly people supposed to say? Let us look to the Prayer Book. The clergyman is suppose to tell these people, "You have heard also that our Lord Jesus Christ has promised in his gospel to grant all these things that you have prayed for; which promise he, for his part, will most surely keep and perform. Therefore, after this promise made by Christ, this infant must also faithfully, for his part, promise by you that are his sureties (until he comes of age to take it upon himself) that he will renounce the devil and all his works, and constantly believe God's holy Word, and obediently keep his commandments." This small child is to promise to do this, or more truly others are to take upon themselves to promise, and even vow that he shall do so. But we must not break the quotation, and therefore let us return to the Prayer Book. "I demand therefore, do you, in the name of this child, renounce the devil and all his works, the vain pomp and glory of the world, with all covetous desires of the same, and the carnal desires of the flesh, so that you will not follow, nor be led by them?" Answers "I renounce them all." That is to say, on the name and behalf of this tender infant about to be baptized, these godly people, these enlightened Christian people, these who know better, who are not dupes, who know all the while that they are promising impossibilities—renounce on behalf of this child what they find it very hard to renounce for themselves—"all covetous desires of the world and the carnal desires of the flesh, so that they will not follow nor be led by them." How can they harden their faces to utter such a false promise, such a mockery of renunciation before the presence of the Father Almighty?

Might not angels weep as they hear the awful promise uttered? Then in the presence of high heaven they profess on behalf of this child that he steadfastly believes the creed, when they know, or might pretty shrewdly judge that the little creature is not yet a steadfast believer in anything, much less in Christ's going down into hell. Notice, they do not say merely that the babe *shall* believe the creed, but they affirm that he does, for they answer in the child's name, "All this I steadfastly believe. Not *we* steadfastly believe," but *I*, the little baby there, unconscious of all their professions and confessions of faith. In answer to the question, "Will you be baptized in this faith?" they reply for the infant, "That is my desire." Surely the infant has no desire in the matter, or at the least, no one has been authorized to declare any desires on the infant's behalf.

But this is not all, for then these godly, intelligent people next promise on the behalf of the infant, that "they shall obediently keep all God's holy will and commandments, and walk in the same all the days of their life." Now, I ask you, dear friends, you who know what true religion means, can you walk in all God's holy commandments yourselves? Dare you make this day a vow on your own part, that you would renounce the devil and all his works, the prideful show and vanities of this wicked world, and all the sinful lusts of the flesh? Dare you, before God, make such a promise as that? You desire such holiness, you earnestly strive after it, but you look for it from God's promise, not from your own. If you dare make such vows I doubt your knowledge of your own hearts and of the spirituality of God's law. But even if you could do this for yourself, would you venture to make such a promise for any other person? For the best-born infant on earth? Come, friends, what do you say? Isn't your reply ready and plain? There isn't room for two opinions among people determined to observe truth in all their ways and words. I can understand a simple, ignorant rustic,[1] who has never learned to read, doing all this at the command of a priest and under the eye of a squire. I can even understand persons doing this when the Reformation was in its dawn, and people

---

1 Rustic—a rural person having a natural simplicity of character or manners.

had newly crept out of the darkness of Popery, but I cannot understand gracious, godly people, standing at the font to insult the all-gracious Father with vows and promises framed upon a fiction, and involving practical falsehood. How dare intelligent believers in Christ to speak words which they know in their conscience to be wickedly aside from truth? When I shall be able to understand the process by which gracious people so accommodate their consciences, even then I shall have a confirmed belief that the God of truth never did and never will confirm a spiritual blessing of the highest order in connection with the utterance of such false promises and untruthful vows. My friends, does it not strike you that declarations so fictitious are not likely to be connected with a new birth brought about by the Spirit of truth?

I am not done with this point, I must take another case, and suppose the sponsors and others to be *ungodly*, and that is no hard supposition, for in many cases we know that godfathers and parents have no more thought of religion than that idolatrous hollowed stone around which they gather. When these sinners have taken their places, what are they about to say? Why, they are about to make the solemn vows I have already recounted in your hearing! Totally irreligious they are, but yet they promise for the baby what they never did, and never thought of doing for themselves—they promise on behalf of this child, "that the child will renounce the devil and all his works, and constantly believe God's holy Word, and obediently keep his commandments." My brothers and sisters, do not think I speak severely here. Really I think there is something here to make mockery for devils. Let every honest person lament, that God's Church should ever tolerate such a thing as this, and that there should be found gracious people who will feel grieved because I, in all kindness of heart, rebuke the atrocity. Unregenerate sinners promising for a poor babe that he shall keep all God's holy commandments which they themselves recklessly break every day! How can anything but the patience of God endure this? What! not speak against it? The very stones in the street might cry out against the infamy of wicked men and women promising that another should renounce the devil and all his works, while they themselves serve the devil and do his works with greediness! As a climax to all this, I am asked to believe that God accepts that wicked promise, and as the result of it, regenerates that child. You cannot believe in regeneration by this operation, whether saints or sinners are the performers. Take them to be godly, then they are wrong for doing what their conscience must condemn. View them as ungodly, and they are wrong for promising what they know they cannot perform, and in neither case can God accept such worship, much less infallibly append regeneration to such a baptism as this.

But you will say "Why do you cry out against it?" I cry out against it because I believe that baptism does not save the soul, and that *the preaching of it has a wrong and evil influence upon people.* We meet with people who, when we tell them that they must be born again, assure us that they were born again when they were baptized. The number of these people is increasing, fearfully increasing, until all grades of society are misled by this belief. How can any man stand up in his pulpit and say, You must be born again to his congregation, when he has already assured them, by his own "unfeigned assent and consent" to it, that they are themselves, every one of them, born again in baptism. What is he to do with them? Why, my dear friends, the gospel then has no voice. They have rammed this ceremony down its throat and it cannot speak to rebuke sin. The person who has been baptized or sprinkled says, "I *am* saved, I *am* a member of Christ, a child of God, and an inheritor of the kingdom of heaven. Who are you, that you should rebuke *me?* Call *me* to repentance? Call *me* to a new life? What better life can I have? for I *am* a member of Christ—a part of Christ's body. What! rebuke *me?* I am a child of God. Can't you see it in my face? No matter what my walk and conversation is, I am a child of God. Moreover, I am an inheritor of the kingdom of heaven. It is true, I drink and swear, and all that, but you know I am an inheritor of the kingdom of heaven, for when I die, though I live in constant sin, you will put me in the grave, and tell everybody that I died 'in sure and certain hope of the resurrection to eternal life.'"

Now, what can be the influence of such preaching as this on our beloved England? Upon my dear and blessed country? Nothing but the worst of ills? If I hadn't loved her, but loved myself most, I might be silent here, but loving England, I cannot and dare not. Having soon to give an account before my God, whose servant I hope I am, I must free myself from this evil as well as from every other, or else on my head may be the doom of souls.

Here let me bring in another point. It is a most fearful fact, that *in no age since the Reformation has Popery made such fearful strides in England as during the last few years*. I had comfortably believed that Popery was only feeding itself upon foreign subscriptions,[1] upon a few titled perverts, and imported monks and nuns. I dreamed that its progress was not real. In fact, I have often smiled at the alarm of many of my brethren at the progress of Popery. But, my dear friends, we have been mistaken, grievously mistaken. If you will read a valuable paper in the magazine called "Christian

1 Subscription—formal assent to the Thirty-nine Articles and the Book of Common Prayer.

Work," those of you who are not acquainted with it will be perfectly startled at its revelations. This great city is now covered with a network of monks, and priests, and sisters of mercy, and the conversions made are not by ones or twos, but by scores, until England is being regarded as the most hopeful spot for Romish missionary enterprise in the whole world. At the present moment there is not a mission which is succeeding anything to the extent which the English mission is. I covet not their money, I despise their sophistries, but I marvel at the way in which they gain their funds for the erection of their ecclesiastical buildings. It really is an alarming matter to see so many of our countrymen going off to that superstition which as a nation we once rejected, and which it was supposed we should never receive again. Popery is making advances such as you would never believe, though a spectator should tell it to you. Close to your very doors, perhaps even in your own houses, you may have evidence before long of what a march Romanism[1] is making. And to what is it to be ascribed? I say, with every ground of probability, that there is no marvel that Popery should increase when you have two things to make it grow—first of all, the falsehood of those who profess a faith which they do not believe, which is quite contrary to the honesty

1 Romanism—the tenets of the Church of Rome; the Roman Catholic religion.

of the Romanist, who does through evil report and good report hold his faith. Then you have—secondly, this form of error known as baptismal regeneration, and commonly called Puseyism,[1] which is not only Puseyism, but Church-of-Englandism, because it is in the Prayer Book, as plainly as words can express it—you have this baptismal regeneration preparing stepping-stones to make it easy for men to go to Rome. I have but to open my eyes a little to foresee Romanism rampant everywhere in the future, since its germs are spreading everywhere in the present. In one of our courts of legislature last Tuesday, the Lord Chief Justice showed his superstition, by speaking of "the risk of the calamity of children dying unbaptized!" Among Dissenters you see a veneration for structures, a modified belief in the sacredness of places, which is idolatry, for to believe in the sacredness of anything but of God and of his own Word, is to idolize, whether it is to believe in the sacredness of the men, the priests, or in the sacredness of the bricks and mortar, or of the fine linen, or what not, which you may use in the worship of God. I see this coming up everywhere—a belief in ceremony, a resting in ceremony, a veneration for altars, fonts,

---

1 Puseyism—the principles of Dr. Pusey and others at Oxford, England, as exhibited in various publications, especially in a series which appeared from 1833 to 1841, designated "Tracts for the Times"; tractarianism.

and Churches—a veneration so profound that we must not venture on a remark, or immediately we are chief of sinners. Here is the essence and soul of Popery, peeping up under the garb of a decent respect for sacred things. It is impossible for the Church of Rome not to spread, when we who are the watch-dogs of the fold are silent, and others are gently and smoothly paving the road, and making it as soft and smooth as possible, that converts may travel down to the lowest hell of Popery. We want John Knox back again. Do not talk to me of mild and gentle men, of soft manners and squeamish words, we want the fiery Knox, and even though his vehemence should "ding our pulpits into blads,"[1] it would be suitable if he roused our hearts to action. We want Luther to tell men and women the truth unmistakably, in simple words. The velvet has got into our ministers' mouths lately, but we must unrobe ourselves of soft clothing, and truth must be spoken, and nothing but truth, for of all lies which have dragged millions down to hell, I look upon this as being one of the most atrocious—that in a Protestant Church there should be found those who swear that baptism saves the soul. Call a person a Baptist, or a Presbyterian, or a Dissenter, or a Churchman, that is nothing to me—if they say that baptism saves the soul, they are wrong, they are in error, they state what God never taught, what the

1 "Ding the pulpit into blads"—break the pulpit into bits.

Bible never laid down, and what should never be maintained by people who profess that the Bible, and the whole Bible, is the religion of Protestants.

I have spoken for awhile now, and there will be some who will say—spoken for awhile very bitterly. Very well, be it so. Medicine is often bitter, but it shall work well. The physician is not bitter because his medicine is so, or if he is evaluated so, it won't matter, so long as the patient is cured. At all events, it is no business of the patient whether the physician is bitter or not, his business is with his own soul's health. There is the truth, and I have told it to you, and if there should be one among you, or if there should be one among the readers of this sermon when it is printed, who is resting on baptism, or resting upon ceremonies of any sort, I implore you, shake off this venomous faith into the fire as Paul did the viper which fastened on his hand. I pray you do not rest on baptism.

> "No outward forms can make you clean,
> The leprosy lies deep within."[1]

I urgently ask you to remember that you must have a new heart and a right spirit, and baptism cannot give you these. You must turn from your sins and follow after Christ. You must have such a faith

---

1 A quote from *Lord, I Am Vile, Conceived in Sin* by Isaac Watts.

as shall make your life holy and your speech devout, or else you do not have the faith of God's elect, and into God's kingdom you shall never come. I pray that you never rest upon this miserable and rotten foundation, this deceitful invention of antichrist. May God save you from it, and bring you to seek the true rock of refuge for weary souls.

I come with much brevity, and I hope with much earnestness, in the second place, to say that FAITH IS THE INDISPENSABLE REQUISITE TO SALVATION. "Whoever *believes* and is baptized will be saved, but whoever does not *believe* will be condemned." Faith is the one indispensable requisite for salvation. This faith is the gift of God. It is the work of the Holy Spirit. Some people don't believe on Jesus. They do not believe because they are not of Christ's sheep, as he himself said to them; "My sheep listen to my voice; I know them, and they follow me. I give them eternal life, and they shall never perish; no one can snatch them out of my hand."[1] What is this believing? Believing consists in two things—*first there is an accrediting of the testimony of God* concerning his Son. God tells you that his Son came into the world and was made flesh, that he lived upon earth for men's sake, that after having spent his life in holiness he was offered up a propitiation for sin, that upon the cross there and then, he made expiation—so made expiation

1 John 10:27–28 (NIV).

for the sins of the world that "Whoever believes in him shall not perish but have eternal life."[1] If you would be saved, you must accredit this testimony which God gives concerning his own Son. Having received this testimony, the next thing is to *confide in it*—indeed here lies, I think, the essence of saving faith, to rest yourself for eternal salvation upon the atonement and the righteousness of Jesus Christ, to be done once for all with all reliance on feelings or on actions, and to trust in Jesus Christ and in what he did for your salvation.

This is faith—the receiving of the truth of Christ—first knowing it to be true, and then acting on that belief. Such a faith as this—such real faith as this makes the person from this time forward hate sin. How can they love the thing which made the Savior bleed? It makes them live in holiness. How can they but seek to honor that God who has loved them so much as to give his Son to die for them. This faith is spiritual in its nature and effects. It operates on the entire person. It changes their heart, enlightens their judgment, and subdues their will. It subjects them to God's supremacy, and makes them receive God's Word as a little child, willing to receive the truth upon the *ipse dixit*[2] of the divine One. It sanctifies their intellect, and makes them willing to be taught God's Word. It cleanses within;

1 See John 3:16 (NIV).
2 Ipse dixit—Latin for "He, himself, said it."

it makes clean the inside of the cup and platter. It beautifies the outside; it makes clean the exterior conduct and the inner motive, so that the person, if their faith is true and real, becomes from this time forward another person from what they ever were before.

Now that such a faith as this should save the soul, is I believe reasonable; yes, more so—it is certain, for we *have seen people saved by it* in this very house of prayer. We have seen the harlot lifted out of the Stygian[1] ditch of her sin, and made an honest woman. We have seen the thief reclaimed. We have known the drunkard in hundreds of instances to be sobered; we have observed faith to work such a change, that all the neighbors who have seen it have gazed and admired, even though they hated it. We have seen faith deliver people in the hour of temptation, and help them to consecrate themselves and their substance to God. We have seen, and hope still to see yet more widely, deeds of heroic consecration to God and displays of witness-bearing against the common current of the times, which have proved to us that faith does affect the person, does save the soul. My hearers, if you would be saved, you must believe in the Lord Jesus Christ. Let me urge you with all my heart to look nowhere but to Christ crucified for your salvation. If you

---

1 Stygian—of the Styx River; figuratively an extremely dark and gloomy place. (From an ancient myth.)

rest on any ceremony—though it is not baptism—
if you rest on any other than Jesus Christ, you must
perish, as surely as this Book is true! I pray that
you do not believe every spirit, but though I, or an
angel from heaven, preach any other doctrine than
this, let him be accursed, for this and this alone
is the soul-saving truth which shall regenerate the
world—"Whoever believes and is baptized will be
saved." Away from all the tag-rags, wax candles, and
millinery of Puseyism! away from all the gorgeous
pomp of Popery! away from the fonts of Church-
of-Englandism! we ask you to turn your eyes to that
naked cross, where hangs as a bleeding man the Son
of God.

> "None but Jesus, none but Jesus
> Can do helpless sinners good."[1]

There is life in a look at the crucified; there is
life at this moment for you. Whoever among you
that can believe in the great love of God towards
mankind in Christ Jesus, you shall be saved. If you
can believe that our great Father desires us to come
to him—that he pants for us—that he calls us every
day with the loud voice of his Son's wounds. If you
can believe now that in Christ there is pardon for
<u>transgressions </u>past, and cleansing for years to come;

1 A quote from *Come, Ye Sinners, Poor and Wretched* by
   Joseph Hart.

if you can trust him to save you, you have already the marks of regeneration. The work of salvation is commenced in you, so far as the Spirit's work is concerned. It is finished in you so far as Christ's work is concerned. I would plead with you—lay hold on Jesus Christ. This is *the* foundation—build on it. This is *the* rock of refuge—fly to it. I pray that you fly to it now. Life is short, time speeds on with wings like an eagle. Swift as the dove pursued by the hawk, fly, fly poor sinner, to God's dear Son. Now touch the hem of his garment; now look into that dear face, once marred with sorrows for you; look into those eyes, once shedding tears for you. Trust him, and if you find him false, then you must perish, but false you never will find him while this word stands true, "Whoever believes and is baptized will be saved, but whoever does not believe will be condemned." God give us this vital, essential faith, without which there is no salvation. Baptized, re-baptized, circumcised, confirmed, fed upon sacraments, and buried in consecrated ground—you shall all perish except those that believe in him. The word is clear and plain—a person that does not believe may plead their baptism, may plead anything they like, "but whoever does not believe will be condemned," for that person there is nothing but the wrath of God, the flames of hell, eternal perdition. So Christ declares, and so must it be.

But now to close, there are some who say, "Yes,

but baptism is in the text! Where do you put that?" That shall be another point, and then we shall be done.

THE BAPTISM IN THE TEXT IS ONE EVIDENTLY CONNECTED WITH FAITH. "Whoever believes and is baptized will be saved." It strikes me, there is no supposition here, that anybody would be baptized who did not believe, or if there is such a supposition, it is very clearly laid down that their baptism will be of no use to them, for they will be condemned, baptized or not, unless they believe. The baptism of the text seems to me—my friends, if you differ from me I am sorry for it, but I must hold my opinion and make it known—it seems to me that baptism is connected with, no, directly follows belief. I would not insist too much on the order of the words, but for other reasons, I think that baptism should follow believing. At any rate it effectually avoids the error we have been combating. A person who knows that they are saved by believing in Christ, does not, when they are baptized, lift their baptism into a saving ordinance. In fact, they are the very best protesters against that mistake, because they hold that they have no right to be baptized until they are saved. They bear a testimony against baptismal regeneration in their being baptized as professedly an already regenerate person. Brothers and sisters, the baptism meant here is a baptism connected with faith, and to this baptism I will admit there is very much ascribed in

Scripture. Into that question I am not going, but I do find some very remarkable passages in which baptism is spoken of very strongly. I find this— "And now what are you waiting for? Get up, be baptized and wash your sins away, calling on his name."[1] I find as much as this in other places. I know that believer's baptism itself does not wash away sin, yet it is so the outward sign and emblem of it to the believer, that the thing visible may be described as the thing signified. Just as our Savior said—"This is my body," when it was not his body, but bread. Yet inasmuch as it represented his body, it was fair and right according to the usage of language to say, "Take, eat, this is my body." And so, inasmuch as baptism to the believer represents the washing of sin—it may be called the washing of sin—not that it is so, but that it is to saved souls the outward symbol and representation of what is done by the power of the Holy Spirit, in the person who believes in Christ.

What connection has this baptism with faith? I think it has just this, *baptism is the declaration of faith.* The man was Christ's soldier, but now in baptism he puts on his regimentals. The man believed in Christ, but his faith remained between God and his own soul. In baptism he says to the baptizer, "I believe in Jesus Christ"; he says to the Church, "I unite with you as a believer in the common truths

1 See Acts 22:16 (NIV).

of Christianity"; he says to the onlooker, "Whatever you may do, as for me, I will serve the Lord." It is the declaration of his faith.

Next, we think baptism is also to the believer a *testimony of their faith.* In baptism the person tells the world what they believe. "I am about," they say, "to be buried in water. I believe that the Son of God was metaphorically baptized in suffering; I believe he was literally dead and buried." To rise again out of the water sets forth to all mankind that they believe in the resurrection of Christ. There is a showing forth in the Lord's Supper of Christ's death, and there is a showing forth in baptism of Christ's burial and resurrection. It is a type, a sign, a symbol, a mirror to the world; a mirror in which religion is as it were reflected. We say to the onlooker, when they ask what is the meaning of this ordinance, "We mean to set forth our faith that Christ was buried, and that he rose again from the dead, and we declare this death and resurrection to be the ground of our trust."

Again, baptism is also *Faith taking her proper place.* It is, or should be one of her first acts of obedience. Reason looks at baptism, and says, "Perhaps there is nothing in it; it cannot do me any good." "True," says Faith, "and therefore will I observe it. If it did me some good my selfishness would make me do it, but inasmuch as to my sense there is no good in it, since I am directed by my Lord so as to fulfill all righteousness, it is my first public declaration that a thing which looks to be unreasonable and seems to be unprofitable, being commanded by God, is law, is law to me. If my Master had told me to pick up six stones and lay them in a row I would do it, without demanding of them, 'What good will it do?' *Cui bono?*[1] is no fit question for soldiers of Jesus. The very simplicity and apparent uselessness of the ordinance should make the believer say, 'Therefore I do it because it becomes the better test to me of my obedience to my Master.'" When you tell your servant to do something, and they cannot comprehend it, if they turn around and say, "Please, sir, what for?" you are quite certain that they hardly understand the relation between master and servant. So when God tells me to do a thing, if I say, "What for?" I cannot have taken the place which Faith should occupy, which is that of simple obedience to whatever the Lord has said. Baptism is commanded, and Faith obeys because it is commanded, and so takes her proper place.

Once more, *baptism is a refreshment to Faith.* While we are made up of body and soul as we are, we shall need some means by which the body shall sometimes be stirred up to co-work with the soul. In the Lord's Supper my faith is assisted by the outward and visible sign. In the bread and in the wine I see no superstitious mystery, I see nothing but bread

1 Cui bono—Latin for "with benefit to whom?"

and wine, but in that bread and wine I do see an assistant to my faith. Through the sign my faith sees the thing signified. So in baptism there is no mysterious efficacy in the baptistry or in the water. We attach no reverence to the one or to the other, but we do see in the water and in the baptism such an assistance as brings home to our faith most manifestly our being buried with Christ, and our rising again in newness of life with him. Explain baptism as such, dear friends, and there is no fear of Popery rising out of it. Explain it so, and we cannot suppose any soul will be led to trust it, but it takes its proper place among the ordinances of God's house. To lift it up in the other way, and say people are saved by it— my friends, how much mischief that one falsehood has done and may do, eternity alone will disclose! If only another George Fox would spring up in all his quaint simplicity and rude honesty to rebuke the idol-worship of this age; to rail at their holy bricks and mortar, holy lecterns, holy alters, holy surplices, right reverend fathers, and I know not what. These things are not holy. God is holy; his truth is holy; holiness belongs not to the carnal and the material, but to the spiritual. If only a trumpet-tongue would cry out against the superstition of the age. I cannot, as George Fox did, give up baptism and the Lord's Supper, but I would infinitely sooner do it, counting it the smaller mistake of the two than perpetrate and assist in perpetrating the uplifting of baptism and the Lord's Supper out of their proper place. My beloved friends, the comrades of my struggles and witnessing, cling to the salvation of faith, and detest the salvation of priests. If I am not mistaken, the day will come when we shall have to fight for a simple spiritual religion far more than we do now. We have been cultivating friendship with those who are either unscriptural in creed or else dishonest, who either believe baptismal regeneration, or profess that they do, and swear before God that they do when they do not. The time is come when there shall be no more truce or parley between God's servants and the timeservers.[1] The time is come when those who follow God must follow God, and those who try to trim and dress themselves and find out a way which is pleasing to the flesh and gentle to carnal desires, must go their way. A great winnowing time is coming to God's saints, and we shall be more set apart one of these days than we are now from union with those who are upholding Popery, under the pretense of teaching Protestantism. We shall be free, I say, from those who teach salvation by baptism, instead of salvation by the blood of our blessed Master, Jesus Christ. May the Lord gird up your loins.[2] Believe me, it is no trifle. It may be that on this ground

---

1 Timeserver—one who adapts their opinions and manners to the times.

2 Gird up your loins—figuratively means "to prepare for action."

Armageddon shall be fought. Here shall come the great battle between Christ and his saints on the one hand, and the world, and forms, and ceremonies, on the other. If we are overcome here, there may be years of blood and persecution, and tossing to and fro between darkness and light, but if we are brave and bold, and do not flinch here, but stand to God's truth, the future of England may be bright and glorious. May we have a truly reformed Church in England, and a godly race to maintain it! The world's future depends on it under God, for in proportion as truth is marred at home, truth is maimed abroad. Out of any system which teaches salvation by baptism must spring infidelity, an infidelity which the false Church already seems willing to nourish and foster beneath her wing. God save this favored land from the brood of her own established religion. Brothers and sisters, stand fast in the liberty by which Christ has made you free, and do not be afraid of any sudden fear or calamity when it comes, for the person who trusts in the Lord, mercy shall surround them, and the person who is faithful to God and Christ shall hear it said at the last, "Well done, good and faithful servant! . . . Come and share your master's happiness!"[1] May the Lord bless this word for Christ's sake.

[Note.—Having been informed that the whole of

1 See Matthew 25:23 (NIV).

the burial service is not usually read at executions,
I have, for the sake of fairness, altered the passage
upon page 318 [in the author's edition], although
it strikes me that I might justly have retained it,
since the rubric of the Church and not the practice of some of its ministers is that with which we
must deal. The rubric says, "The office ensuing
is not to be used for any that die unbaptized, or
excommunicate, or have laid violent hands upon
themselves." The victim of our capital punishment
is not by this rubric shut out from the privileges (?)
of the Anglican burial service, unless his condemna-
tion may be viewed as tantamount to excommuni-
cation, which I can hardly think is the case, since
many condemned people receive the sacrament. I
have also altered an incorrect expression on page
316, which has been pointed out to me by both
friends and foes. May God grant that the contro-
versy which this sermon has commenced may lead
to the advancement of his truth, and the enlightenment of many.]

NOTES

NOTES

NOTES

MAN'S QUESTIONS & GOD'S ANSWERS

Am I accountable to God?
Each of us will give an account of himself to God. ROMANS 14:12 (NIV).

Has God seen all my ways?
Everything is uncovered and laid bare before the eyes of him to whom we must give account. HEBREWS 4:13 (NIV).

Does he charge me with sin?
But the Scripture declares that the whole world is a prisoner of sin. GALATIANS 3:22 (NIV).
All have sinned and fall short of the glory of God. ROMANS 3:23 (NIV).

Will he punish sin?
The soul who sins is the one who will die. EZEKIEL 18:4 (NIV).
For the wages of sin is death, but the gift of God is eternal life in Christ Jesus our Lord. ROMANS 6:23 (NIV).

Must I perish?
He is patient with you, not wanting anyone to perish, but everyone to come to repentance. 2 PETER 3:9 (NIV).

How can I escape?
Believe in the Lord Jesus, and you will be saved. ACTS 16:31 (NIV).

Is he able to save me?
Therefore he is able to save completely those who come to God through him. HEBREWS 7:25 (NIV).

Is he willing?
Christ Jesus came into the world to save sinners. 1 TIMOTHY 1:15 (NIV).

Am I saved on believing?
Whoever believes in the Son has eternal life, but whoever rejects the Son will not see life, for God's wrath remains on him. JOHN 3:36 (NIV).

Can I be saved now?
Now is the time of God's favor, now is the day of salvation. 2 CORINTHIANS 6:2 (NIV).

As I am?
Whoever comes to me I will never drive away. JOHN 6:37 (NIV).

Shall I not fall away?
Him who is able to keep you from falling. JUDE 1:24 (NIV).

If saved, how should I live?
Those who live should no longer live for themselves but for him who died for them and was raised again. 2 CORINTHIANS 5:15 (NIV).

What about death and eternity?
I am going there to prepare a place for you. I will come back and take you to be with me that you also may be where I am. JOHN 14:2-3 (NIV).